I0453170

Seeds of Strength

Affirmations and Life Lessons from a Black Woman
Who Transformed Her Story

By Kendra Garden

Copyright © 2025

All rights reserved.

This is a work of nonfiction. All characters and descriptions of events are the product of the author's imagination and any resemblance to actual persons is entirely coincidental. The information in this book expresses the author's views and opinions and does not necessarily represent the views of any organization.

First published 2025

Dedication Page

For my sons —

You are the reason I chose strength over surrender, and hope over fear. Every seed I've planted in this book was first inspired by the love I hold for you.

May you always remember that even in life's hardest seasons, you carry the power to bloom.

Acknowledgments Page

I would not be the woman I am today without the presence, lessons, and love of those who have walked beside me.

To my family — thank you for teaching me resilience. Every challenge, every blessing, and every sacrifice became the foundation of the story I share here.

To my friends and sisters in spirit — your encouragement has been a constant reminder that I am never alone on this journey. Thank you for listening to my dreams, speaking life into me, and reminding me to keep pressing forward.

To my mentors — those who have guided me both professionally and personally — thank you for planting seeds of wisdom that have grown into my purpose.

And to every reader holding this book in your hands — thank you. Your willingness to join me in these pages is proof that stories matter, and that transformation is possible for us all.

Table Of Contents

Dedication Page..3

Acknowledgments Page 4

Introduction: Welcome to Your Power 6

Chapter 1: Roots of Struggle 7

Chapter 2: Teenage Motherhood 11

Chapter 3: Education and Perseverance 14

Chapter 4: Love, Loss, and Awakening 16

Chapter 5:   Breaking Cycles 20

Chapter 6: A New Beginning 22

Chapter 7: A New Kind of Love 25

Chapter 8: Becoming the Woman I Was Meant to Be 27

Chapter 9: Affirmations and Daily Practices 29

Chapter 10: Closing 34

About the Author 39

Closing Words 40

Continue Your Journey 41

Your Seeds of Strength Journal 42

Notes & Reflections 43

My Daily Affirmations 45

Seeds Yet to Bloom 46

Introduction

Welcome to Your Power

This is not just a book of affirmations. This is my story. A story of survival, resilience, and transformation.

It's the story of a little girl who grew up peeing in a bucket.
The story of a teenager raising a baby before she was even grown herself.
The story of a woman who endured heartbreak after heartbreak, yet refused to let those hardships define her forever.

As you read, know this isn't written from a place of perfection. I don't stand above you as someone who has it all figured out. I am a woman who has walked through the fire, who has cried herself to sleep, who has questioned her worth, and who has fought tooth and nail for a better life — for herself and for her children.

This book is my offering. My hand reaching out to yours. My hope is that through my story and these affirmations, you will see yourself more clearly, love yourself more deeply, and believe in the power that already lives inside you.

Chapter 1

Roots of Struggle

I was born to a 15-year-old mother and a 17-year-old father. From the very beginning, my life was marked by instability. They left me in the care of my grandmother at birth. My father would drop in randomly, making promises he never kept, always ending in disappointment. Sometimes whole years would pass before he showed up again — usually with another lie that lifted my hopes high, only to let them crash back down.

Everyone around me would say, *"You look just like him."* And I often wondered: if I looked like him, why didn't he want me? That question stayed with me through much of my childhood, and truthfully, it still lingers even today. Each time he appeared, I felt a flicker of hope — only for it to be crushed the moment he disappeared again.

My earliest memories are not of toys or playgrounds, but of survival. For many years, until I was about eleven or twelve, we had no working plumbing. We used a single bucket for everyone in the house — to pee and poop in. That memory stayed with me, *heavy and raw, shaping how I viewed myself and the world.*

Life at home was poor, but we had a rhythm — a survival routine that shaped me. Saturdays were not for cartoons or sleepovers like I imagined other kids had. For us, Saturdays started before daylight. We'd be at the laundromat as soon as the doors opened, loading machines with piles of clothes. After that came chores — watering plants, raking the yard, deep-cleaning the house — all before we were ever allowed to play. I wasn't allowed to have friends sleep over anyway. The bucket was our family's private reality, and I carried that embarrassment heavily. So outside became my world, the only place where I could breathe, imagine, and just be a child.

Me as a child. "She carried questions, struggles, and dreams — but also the seeds of strength."

My grandmother was a strong but stern woman. She demanded discipline, and in her house, discipline often came with the sting of a leather belt. I still remember one whooping that stayed with me all my life. I interrupted an adult conversation, and my grandmother whipped me hard to teach me that children didn't cut into grown folks' talk. She used a leather belt — the kind Whoopi Goldberg used to sharpen a razor in *The Color Purple*. I can still see the welts it left on my skin, a reminder of pain and silence.

I often felt like I was blamed for everything. Being the oldest among my sisters and cousins she was raising, the heaviest punishments seemed to fall on me. We had to hold our small, tender hands out as she struck them with the belt. The pain stung so badly that we would switch hands for a moment of relief, tears streaming as we begged her to stop. If we couldn't hold our hands out any longer, or if we pulled back before she was finished, the belt would land wherever it fell — arms, legs, wherever it struck.

At the time, it felt unbearable. Yet even in those painful memories, I carry no hatred. I forgave her a long time ago. She was doing the only thing she knew, and in her own way, she believed she was preparing us for life. She worked hard and cared for us the best way she could. I love that woman with every bone in me. And though it came with pain, she shaped so much of the woman I am still becoming today.

As a child, I also carried the wound of colorism. My sisters were light-skinned, considered "better" or "prettier" by society's standards. I was darker, chocolate-skinned, and often reminded of it through cruel words. People called me "black" in a way that was meant to wound, not uplift. For years, I felt less than — unworthy. And yet, when I look back at photos of myself now, I see that I was a beautiful little chocolate girl all along — I just didn't know it or feel it back then.

My summers weren't spent carefree. From a young age, I worked alongside my grandmother to earn money for school clothes and the things I needed. It was tough, and sometimes it felt like childhood slipped away before I ever had the chance to hold onto it.

I didn't know it at the time, but the roots of strength were being planted in me — roots that would carry me through the storms to come.

Chapter 2

Teenage Motherhood

By the time I was about fourteen, I met the father of my first child through one of my older cousins. We all went to the same high school. At sixteen, I became pregnant — and that changed everything. At that age, I didn't even know what love really was. I wasn't in love; I was searching for belonging, for someone to choose me, for a place where I felt wanted. I thought I had found that in my child's father.

But being a teenage mother meant I missed out on so many of the things most high school girls look forward to. I didn't get to go to pep rallies, dances, or have a prom night to remember. While my classmates were laughing in the bleachers and dressing up for school events, I was already carrying a weight far heavier than my years.

Because of the pregnancy, I had to transfer to an all-girls school designed for pregnant teens and young mothers. When I walked across the stage at graduation, I had my three-month-old baby boy on my hip. I was seventeen years old, holding my diploma in one hand and my son in the other.

For a short while, his father and I made plans. We were going to move in together after my graduation. But before we could take that step, he got caught up in a street gunfight and ended up in prison. Just like that, I was left alone to raise my son, and it marked the beginning of the toxic relationships that would follow.

When my child's father went to prison, I was suddenly left to raise my son on my own. I remember the fear that came with living by myself for the first time. I was seventeen, in my own apartment, with a baby boy. Every sound at night seemed louder. Every decision carried more weight because it wasn't just about me anymore — it was about survival. I had to figure out how to make a home, how to put food on the table, and how to be strong even when I felt scared and broken inside.

Those years forced me to grow up quickly, but they also planted seeds of resilience. I learned to push forward, even when my heart felt heavy and the path ahead seemed uncertain.

Motherhood grew my backbone, but it also revealed my broken beliefs. I wanted love, I wanted security, but the men I was drawn to back then couldn't give me either. What I didn't understand yet was how much my own thoughts — the ones buried deep in my subconscious — were shaping the choices I made. Negative beliefs like *I am not enough. I don't deserve better. Life will always be a struggle.* They played like background music in my mind, and I didn't even realize I was dancing to that tune.

I worked hard to keep a roof over our heads, but it was always a struggle. There were times I didn't have consistent car insurance. Times I had to choose between paying one bill or another, constantly robbing Peter to pay Paul just to stay afloat. The stress was relentless, but I pushed forward because I had to.

I still remember the pride of buying my very first car. To me, it meant freedom — a way to get to work, to carry my baby where he needed to go, to feel like I was finally standing on my own two feet. But the reality was, even gas money was a struggle. One day, desperate and late for work, a friend and I made a foolish choice. We siphoned gas. I thought we were being slick, but I had on my work shirt — my name and job stitched right across my chest for the world to see. It wasn't long before the cops showed up.

The embarrassment I felt in that moment cut deep. I wanted to sink into the ground. I was young, broke, trying to keep it all together, and instead I got caught in one of my lowest decisions. Looking back now, I see it as one of those lessons life burned into me — shame turned into a kind of fuel that kept me pushing toward something better.

If you are reading this with a baby on your hip, or with bills spread out in front of you, I want you to know this: you are not alone. And the strength you are building in this very moment will one day reveal itself as the foundation for the life you deserve.

Every sleepless night, every overdue notice, every tear you wipe away in silence is not wasted. It is shaping you. It is proof that you are already stronger than you think. The world may try to tell you that you are behind, but I promise — you are right on time for your own story.

Hold on to the truth that what feels like survival today will grow into wisdom tomorrow. You are planting seeds of resilience with every hard choice you make, and those seeds will bloom into a life far greater than what you can see right now.

Chapter 3

Education and Perseverance

Even in the middle of raising children, enduring heartbreak, and trying to make ends meet, I never stopped chasing growth. Education became a pathway that helped me see beyond my immediate struggles.

It took long nights, early mornings, and sacrifices that sometimes felt impossible. But every step was proof to myself that I was capable of more than the world — and even I — had once believed.

Balancing motherhood, work, and school was no small task. There were days I was at my breaking point, running on little to no sleep, just trying to make it all work. I had moments where I wondered if I was fooling myself, if I was trying to reach too high. But with each completed class, each certificate earned, each new skill learned, I was breaking through barriers that had once felt unshakable.

Even as I poured myself into my career, the weight of my toxic marriage pressed on me daily. I was determined not to let it stop me, but deep down I knew something had to change. Those years gave me both strength and scars — and eventually, they led me to a breaking point I could no longer ignore.

Education didn't solve all my problems, but it gave me something I had longed for: confidence. It reminded me that no matter what I had been through, I had the power to rise, to learn, and to transform my future.

For a while, I believed I had finally built the foundation I always wanted. I was working, raising my son, and walking with a degree and license in hand — proof that the girl who had once been counted out could, in fact, create something steady. I thought this stability would be the springboard into the next chapter of my life.

But life has a way of testing even our strongest foundations. As I stepped into marriage, I thought I had found security and love that would last. What I didn't know then was that this chapter of perseverance in school was only preparing me for the battles of the heart that were still ahead.

Chapter 4

Love, Loss, and Awakening

When my marriage finally ended, the silence was almost too much to take in. On one hand, it was heavy. I could feel the weight of everything I had just walked away from pressing in on me. On the other hand, it was freeing. For the first time in years, there was no arguing, no tension waiting for me when I walked through the door, no tightness in my chest from living in a home that felt more like a battlefield than a safe place.

The chapter was closed. And there I was, standing in the middle of my life with no clear direction forward. For so long, I had worked myself to the bone trying to hold everything together. I kept telling myself, *If I just love harder, work harder, pray harder, maybe things will change.* But they didn't. Divorce was the very thing I feared the most, and yet it became the only doorway left open for me to walk through.

On the outside, it looked like things were coming together. I was pursuing my education, I was working, I was checking off the boxes I thought would make me whole. But inside, the cracks were widening. Instead of safety, I found myself shrinking. Instead of love, I felt the weight of constant tension. Slowly, I lost pieces of myself until I barely recognized the woman I had become.

That realization didn't come all at once. It came in whispers — in the moments when I caught myself pretending, in the nights I cried alone, in the mornings I forced myself to smile even though my spirit felt empty. Looking back now, I see it so clearly: what I called "stability" was really survival. And survival is not the same as peace.

At first, the silence after divorce was deafening. I had to relearn how to live without the constant noise of conflict, without the daily weight of someone else's unhappiness pressing into my spirit. I had to face the loneliness of my own company, and the questions that surfaced when the distractions were gone: *Who am I now? What do I really want? Where do I go from here?*

The only answer I had in those first few weeks was simple: fall into God. That was the only thing I knew to do. When everything else was stripped away — the marriage, the expectations, the roles I thought I was supposed to play — His presence became the one steady thing in my life. I cried, I prayed, I poured my heart out, and I let Him hold the pieces of me that felt too broken to carry alone. Looking back, I know this was the very beginning of my awakening. I didn't call it that at the time. All I knew was that God was pulling me closer, reminding me that I had never been alone, not even in my lowest moments.

But just because I was leaning on God didn't mean things instantly got easy. Life after divorce came with a whole new set of struggles. The bills didn't stop coming just because I was now the only one responsible for paying them. My youngest son still needed me — he needed stability, love, and consistency, even when I was running on fumes. There were nights I cried myself to sleep because the loneliness felt like it would swallow me whole. There were days I questioned if I had made the right decision, wondering if maybe it would have been easier to just stay and keep enduring.

Not long after the split, I faced another test — this time from the woman my husband had chosen. Rather than allowing me the space to heal and move on, she seemed determined to pull me into her bitterness. She monitored my social media closely, sending messages at all hours and even creating new accounts whenever the old ones were reported and blocked. She posted pictures, left comments on my family members' pages, and did everything she could to get under my skin.

It didn't stop with me. She even dragged my son into it, mocking and targeting him online. That crossed a line no mother can tolerate. It hurt, but it also revealed something powerful inside me — a determination to protect my peace and my family no matter what.

Eventually, the harassment grew so severe that it had to be handled legally. That was a turning point. I realized I couldn't control how others acted, but I could control how I responded. Instead of breaking me, the situation pushed me to set boundaries, to stand taller, and to lean even harder into God's covering. What was meant to tear me down only made me more unshakable.

And even in the middle of those hard days, something inside me had shifted. I wasn't just surviving anymore. A quiet strength was building in me — the kind that doesn't shout but whispers, *You can do this. You are stronger than you think.*

I started to notice little signs of that strength showing up in everyday moments. Like the first time I paid the bills by myself and realized, *I actually did that.* Or the times I sat across from my youngest son and reassured him, even when I wasn't sure of myself, because I knew he needed to see me standing tall. Those small victories mattered. He reminded me that starting over wasn't just about picking up the pieces — it was about rediscovering myself.

It was in those rediscoveries that I began to see God's hand shaping me. I realized that the very soil watered with tears could also grow new seeds. Seeds of hope. Seeds of faith. Seeds of self-love. My divorce was painful, yes. But it also gave me back something priceless: my voice. It gave me permission to imagine a life built on peace instead of chaos, on love instead of fear.

I won't pretend I had it all figured out. I didn't. There were still days of grief, anger, and confusion. But there were also moments of joy I hadn't felt in years. I laughed with my child and realized we were going to be okay. I sat in the quiet of my room and felt God's presence wrap around me like a blanket. And slowly, I began to see that what once felt like an ending was really the start of my transformation.

This chapter of my life wasn't glamorous. It didn't look like strength from the outside. But it was the kind of strength that grows quietly, like roots deep underground, preparing to break through the surface. Divorce didn't just close a door — it opened space for me to finally see who I was, who I wanted to become, and most importantly, who God had called me to be.

Chapter 5

Breaking Cycles

By this point in my journey, my two oldest sons were already grown and finding their own way. My focus was now on raising my youngest son, the one still under my care, and on being intentional about the example I set for him. I was beginning to understand that my life was not just shaped by what happened to me, but also by the thoughts I carried within me. For years, I had been unconsciously repeating beliefs like *I'm not enough, I'll always struggle, love never lasts for me.* Those thoughts sat deep in my subconscious and quietly influenced every choice I made.

It wasn't until the heartbreak of my divorce and the pressure of raising my youngest son that I finally realized how much power my mind held. I started to pay attention to the things I told myself. Slowly, I began replacing the negative with positive truths.

I learned that breaking cycles isn't just about changing your circumstances — it's about changing your mindset. For me, this meant forgiving my past, even the people who had hurt me most, and choosing not to pass that pain forward to my child.

I wanted to model resilience for my boys, to show them that even when life knocks you down, you can stand up again. I wanted them to know they weren't bound to repeat the struggles they saw me endure. And to do that, I had to believe it for myself first.

Each small shift in my thinking became like a seed planted — seeds of strength, faith, and self-love that I continue to water every day.

Chapter 6

A New Beginning

I began reading books — so many books. Titles like *The Secret* by Rhonda Byrne, *As a Man Thinketh* by James Allen, and *The Power of the Subconscious Mind* by Joseph Murphy. In the world I grew up in, people didn't usually talk about these kinds of ideas, but they resonated deeply with me. I knew I had discovered something big — big for me, big for the way I would see and shape my life.

Once I heard my thoughts clearly, I couldn't unhear them. I started writing them down — the ugly ones, the old ones, the ones that sounded like voices from my past:

I'm too dark to be beautiful.
I'm always the problem.
I'll always struggle.
Love is for other people, not me.

Seeing them on paper wasn't just an eye-opener, it was a soul awakening. For the first time, I began to see myself and my life with clearer eyes. I learned that the subconscious mind doesn't argue — it obeys. If I fed it fear, it would attract fear. If I fed it shame, it would attract more shame. If I wanted a different harvest, I had to plant different seeds.

So I started small, quietly. I wrote down things that felt impossible to believe at first:

I am worthy of being chosen and kept.
I am beautiful in my chocolate-colored skin.
I am safe, provided for, and guided.
Healthy, kind love is for me.
I am capable. I am enough. I am a good mother.

At first, the words felt like clothes that didn't fit. But I kept showing up. I whispered them while washing dishes. I said them while driving. I posted them on social media, wrote them on sticky notes, and prayed them over my life. Slowly but surely, I felt my spirit shift.

Affirmations didn't change my past. They changed my posture. They taught me to speak to myself like someone I loved.

Life had taught me hard lessons, but it was also beginning to show me that renewal was possible. Out of the storms, I started to rebuild, piece by piece.

I had been through toxic relationships, heartbreak, and the constant pressure of survival. Yet each experience planted something in me — a lesson, a boundary, a deeper understanding of who I was becoming.

By now, I was not the same scared teenage mother, nor the brokenhearted young woman trying to make sense of her pain. I was evolving into someone stronger, more aware, and more determined to live differently.

It wasn't an overnight change. Healing never is. But little by little, I felt myself growing into the woman I was meant to be. I was learning to stop defining myself by what I had lost, and instead by what I had survived.

This chapter of my life wasn't about perfection — it was about progress. And for the first time, I felt a glimpse of hope that maybe, just maybe, the life I had longed for was within reach.

Chapter 7
A New Kind of Love

After years of heartbreak and lessons, love found me in a different way. This time, it wasn't chaos or struggle — it was steady, respectful, and kind. I met the man who would become my husband, and with him came a new kind of partnership.

What drew me to him wasn't only his charm or the way he carried himself, but also how different he was from what I had known before. He didn't push for sex before marriage — instead, he wanted stability, a family, and to prove himself as a provider. That was rare, and it felt special.

At the same time, I can admit it wasn't easy. He was handsome, sexy, and so full of confidence. After going without intimacy for so long, the pull was there. But the fact that he valued building a foundation first left an impression on me — it showed me a different kind of love, one rooted in commitment and responsibility.

He wasn't the type of man I had been drawn to in the past. He carried himself with dignity, worked hard, and earned respect in his career as a crew leader at a well-known boatyard company. More importantly, he treated me with the affection and care I had always longed for but never truly received.

Being with him showed me that love didn't have to hurt. It didn't have to come with betrayal or insecurity. It could be nurturing, warm, and safe. For the first time, I felt what it was like to be with someone who wanted my peace as much as I did.

He may not practice affirmations the way I do, but he supports me. He watches from afar, proud that I am studying, learning, and growing. He celebrates that I share these lessons with others. His quiet encouragement gives me the space to keep becoming the woman I was meant to be.

Healthy love didn't rescue me. It met me — whole and growing — and chose me there.

Chapter 8

Becoming the Woman I Was Meant to Be

Motherhood, heartbreak, and survival shaped me, but they didn't define me. What defined me was my decision to rise above it all — to take the pain and use it as fuel for growth.

By this stage of my journey, I was no longer just surviving. I was becoming. I was the mother of three sons — two grown and one still at home.

When I take inventory of my life now, I see a different story unfolding. I earned a management degree and completed a nursing program to become a licensed nurse. I became a professional life coach and am pursuing my master coach certification so I can help others walk this same path of renewing the mind and transforming the heart. I consider myself a social media inspirator and a woman who naturally "coaches" the girls and women I encounter in everyday life. And now, through this book, I'm sharing my story fully for the first time.

I don't pretend my past didn't happen. I honor it by telling the truth and choosing a different truth today. The bucket, the broken promises, the colorism, the welts, the loneliness, the late notices, the heartbreak — none of it was the end of me. All of it became soil.

I am proof that when you change your thoughts, you change your life. Not instantly. Not perfectly. But powerfully.

I came to understand that affirmations were not just words — they were seeds. And when planted daily, when spoken with belief, they reshaped not only how I saw myself but also what I believed I could create.

I became a professional life coach because I was already living as one in spirit. On social media, with coworkers, and with women I met in everyday life, I found myself naturally speaking life into them. Encouraging them. Planting seeds in their journeys the way I had learned to plant them in mine.

This book — my story — is the first time I've shared all of this so openly. It is my testimony that no matter how dark the past, there is always a light waiting to be claimed.

Chapter 9

Affirmations and Daily Practices

By now, you've walked with me through the pain, the lessons, and the victories. But I don't want to just leave you with my story. I want to leave you with something you can use in your own life every single day.

Affirmations are more than nice words. They are seeds. Each time you speak one, you're planting something in your mind, and over time, those seeds take root and grow. This is how we begin to shift our subconscious minds — the part of us that quietly drives our choices and our beliefs.

Below are affirmations and practices that I have used personally — the same ones that helped me transform my thinking and, ultimately, my life.

Affirmations for Self-Worth

I am worthy of love, peace, and success.
My value is not determined by my past, but by the truth of who I am today.
I am enough, exactly as I am.
My story matters, and it is still being written.

Affirmations for Healing and Growth

I release what no longer serves me.
I forgive myself and others so that I can live in freedom.
Every day, I am becoming stronger, wiser, and more at peace.
I trust the process of my healing.

Affirmations for Beauty, Health, and Gratitude

I am grateful for my body and all it allows me to do.
I radiate beauty from the inside out.
I honor my health by caring for myself with love.
Each day is a gift, and I choose to live it fully.

Daily Practices

Morning Check-In

Begin your day by speaking three affirmations aloud.

Write down one thing you're grateful for before stepping into the world.

Midday Reset

Take a deep breath and remind yourself: *I am exactly where I need to be.*

If stress rises, pause and replace negative thoughts with one positive truth.

Evening Reflection

Write down one thing you overcame today.

Note one moment that made you smile.

End your day with a gratitude statement: *I am thankful for this day, and I release it with peace.*

Affirmations alone won't change your life. But when spoken with intention, paired with daily practice, and rooted in belief, they transform your inner world — and when your inner world changes, your outer world will always follow.

Chapter 10

Closing

If you've made it this far, I want you to know something powerful: you are stronger than you realize.

This book is the first time I've shared my full story. From a little girl peeing in a bucket, to a teenage mother carrying her baby across the graduation stage, to a woman who has known heartbreak, divorce, struggle, and survival — yet also found healing, purpose, and love.

My journey has shaped me into a nurse, life coach, master coach in progress, social media inspirator, and an empowered wife, walking boldly in love and purpose.

I pour encouragement into women and girls I meet. That, too, is part of my calling. My hope is that my story and these affirmations have planted something inside you — a seed of belief, of courage, of possibility.

You don't have to wait for someone else to save you. The power to shift your life is already within you. Your thoughts are the soil. Your words are the seeds. And your actions are the water that will make them grow.

So walk boldly. Speak kindly to yourself. And never forget: you were made for more.

Affirmations for Seeds of Strength

Chapter 1 – Roots of Struggle

I am worthy of love and new beginnings.
My past does not define me.
Every ending is also a new beginning.

Chapter 2 – Teenage Motherhood

I have the courage to rise from my mistakes.
Every setback is a setup for growth.
I release shame and step into grace.

Chapter 3 – Education and Perseverance

I am not bound by the pain of my past.
I create space for joy, peace, and abundance.
I honor the lessons that shaped me.

Chapter 4 – Love, Loss, and Awakening

I am strong enough to face anything that comes my way.
The challenges I face are the soil where my strength grows.
I am no longer surviving — I am thriving.

Chapter 5 – Breaking Cycles

I am deserving of rest, peace, and renewal.
My mind and body are worthy of care.
Healing is my birthright.

Chapter 6 – A New Beginning

I speak life into myself and others.
The words I affirm become the seeds of my future.
I choose to create my reality with intention.

Chapter 7 – A New Kind of Love

I celebrate my growth at every stage.
I honor the progress I've made and the woman I am becoming.
Transformation is always possible for me.

Chapter 8 – Becoming the Woman I Was Meant to Be

I am becoming the highest version of myself every single day.
My past is not my prison — it is my soil, and I grow stronger from it.
I honor my journey and celebrate my growth.

I am proof that transformation is possible.
My story is not just survival — it is victory.
I was created with purpose, and I walk boldly in it.
I am the woman I was always meant to be.

Seeds of Strength is a memoir of survival, resilience, and transformation. From childhood struggles and teenage motherhood to heartbreak, healing, and new beginnings, this is the raw and inspiring journey of a Black woman who found her voice, her worth, and her power.

Along the way, she shares affirmations and daily practices that helped her shift her mindset and plant the seeds of a stronger future. Her story is not just her own — it's an invitation for you to believe in your own strength and the life you are capable of creating.

About the Author

Kendra Garden is a wife, nurse, professional life coach, and social-media inspirator who helps women renew their minds and transform their hearts. She is passionate about teaching the power of affirmations, mindset, and self-love through her writing and coaching.

She is the author of *Seeds of Strength: Affirmations and Life Lessons from a Black Woman Who Transformed Her Life* and the creator of the *Seeds of Strength 30-Day Affirmation Workbook* — a companion resource designed to guide readers through daily affirmations, journaling, and reflection.

Kendra lives her message of resilience and transformation as the proud mother of three sons. She continues to inspire women through her story, her coaching, and her belief that no matter what the past holds, every woman carries the power to bloom.

Closing Words

If you've made it to this page, I want you to know: you are stronger than you realize. Every word you've read and every affirmation you've spoken has planted a seed of strength within you.

Your story is still unfolding. Each day is another chance to rise, to choose love over fear, faith over doubt, and hope over despair.

Carry these affirmations with you. Water them daily. And watch how beautifully your life begins to bloom.

Always remember: you are worthy, you are powerful, and you are becoming the woman you were always meant to be.

With love and light,
Kendra Garden

Continue Your Journey

The story you've just read is only the beginning. Transformation isn't a one-time event — it's a daily practice.

To help you live these affirmations day by day, I've created the *Seeds of Strength 30-Day Affirmation Workbook.*

This companion resource will guide you through:

> Daily affirmations with space to reflect and write

> Journaling prompts to deepen your growth

> Practical exercises to plant and water the seeds of strength in your own life

Use it alongside this memoir to turn inspiration into action — one day, one page, one seed at a time.

Coming soon — stay connected for updates!

Your Seeds of Strength Journal

This space is for you.

Use these pages to reflect, release, and write your own affirmations. Let your words take root and remind you daily that strength is already within you.

Notes & Reflections

Take a moment to reflect on your own journey. Use these prompts to guide your thoughts:

What parts of my past have become soil for my growth?

Which affirmations speak most deeply to me right now?

How has my definition of strength changed over time?

Where in my life do I need to plant new seeds of belief?

Write your thoughts below:

_____

_____

_____

_____

_____

_____

_____

_____

_____

_____

_____

_____

_____

_____

_____

_____

_____

My Daily Affirmations

Use this space to write affirmations of your own. Speak them daily, and let them grow inside of you like seeds.

_____

_____

_____

_____

_____

_____

_____

_____

_____

_____

_____

_____

_____

_____

Seeds Yet to Bloom

This page is for your private thoughts, dreams, or doodles —
the things that have not yet blossomed, but are waiting within
you.

_____

_____

_____

_____

_____

_____

_____

_____

_____

_____

_____

_____

_____

Connect with Kendra

Thank you for reading Seeds of Strength. My hope is that this book planted seeds of encouragement and growth in your life.

You can stay connected with me here:

Blog: www.seeds-of-strength.com
Facebook: https://www.facebook.com/share/1SAGDGysxg/
Email: Seedsofstrengthbook@gmail.com

Follow along for affirmations, journaling prompts, and updates on new projects. Let's grow through life together.

www.ingramcontent.com/pod-product-compliance
Lightning Source LLC
Chambersburg PA
CBHW051600120626
46551CB00013B/1596